Touch the Sky

"There are magical moments and poetic turns in these big wonderful poems that sing of family, of barrio, of dirt, of work, of play, of celestial dreams... of what it is to be Mexican in the United States—ni de aqui , ni de alla, but always landing on solid ground, proof we belong anywhere. Donato Martinez has concocted an expansive and rich collection."

—Luis J. Rodriguez, author of *Always Running: Mi Vida Loca/Gang Days in L.A.*, *Borrowed Bones: New Poems from the Poet Laureate of Los Angeles*, and *From Our Land to Our Land*

"Donato Martinez's poems bring me joy. Like sitting on a porch hearing your elders tell tales, like relaxing with friends shooting the shit, like the best hip hop of the 90s, like family breakfast on Sunday morning. Pull up a chair and treat yourself."

—Tomas Moniz, author of *Big Familia*

"Donato Martinez successfully gives us back the essence of poetic flow that's been missing from our lives during these uncertain times. His unique style, rhyme and cadence pull me back into the days of giving a damn and living life freely at the same time. Each metaphor serves to bring the reader into Martinez's world of cultura, familia, and comunidad that made him into who he is today. If you've never had days filled with wonderment, fear, laughter, and a sense of urgency all balled into one moment, do yourself a favor and float through his home-grown narration intentionally without pause."

—Dr. Jessica Ayo Alabi, Professor at Orange Coast College, Founder and CEO of Alabi Community Consulting

"In this debut collection of poems, Donato Martinez continues to captivate and inspire. Recalling memories from childhood, he places us in the middle of the lives of a Mexican immigrant family attempting to carve out their little piece of the "American Dream." I could visualize scenes of the barrio where he grew up and feel a close connection to the people who called it home."

—Obed Silva, Professor of English at East Los Angeles College, writer of the memoir, *The Death of My Father the Pope*

"Through his palabras, Donato Martinez presents and pays homage to the many men and women who often are excluded from our history books. He acknowledges their being, their presence, and the many contributions they make to our everyday life. Donato's poems make sure that we recognize their sudor, their hours of excessive work, and understand that they keep our cities in motion."

—Angelina F. Veyna, Emeritus Professor of History, Santa Ana College

"Touch the Sky is a collection of silent prayers told over the beds of sleeping children, dreams of blacktop crossovers, Doritos sandwiches, and the return of Aztec gods. At once modern and ancient, urban, and sacred, Donato Martinez's debut book *Touch the Sky* mines the everyday for the profound. Martinez turns his eye just outside the window and finds heaven in the streets and alleys. This is Chicano city writing. And it's damn good."

—Matt Sedillo, author of *Mowing Leaves of Grass* and *City on the Second Floor*

MARIA –
THANK you so much!

Touch the Sky

LOVE –
DONATO M.

by

Donato Martinez

EL MARTILLO PRESS

EL MARTILLO PRESS

Touch the Sky by Donato Martinez.
©Donato Martinez, 2023. All rights reserved.

Published by El Martillo Press
in the United States of America.
elmartillopress.com

Photos provided by Gabriel Martinez.

Set in Garamond.
Typeset for El Martillo Press by David A. Romero.
davidaromero.com

NOTICE: SCHOOLS AND BUSINESSES
El Martillo Press offers copies of this book at quantity discount with bulk purchase for educational, business, or sales promotional use. For information, please email the publisher at elmartillopress@gmail.com.

To my parents, Mario Martinez and Maria de Jesus Martinez:

For the courage to cross the border, children towing behind, hanging on to their apron strings and shoelaces. You tilled the soil and planted the seeds. I hope you have enjoyed the fruits of your labor and seen your American dream in us, your children.

To my children, Gabriel and Abigail:

You have been my third eye when I have been unable to see clearly. You are a daily reminder of beauty. You took the baton that was handed to you and have never stopped running. Both high school valedictorians and college educated. You are my dream. I love your passion for life. You are the stars on my back. You inspire me to inspire.

CONTENTS

Tough Love

For Broken-Hearted Foos

Coming Up

Foreword

OBED SILVA

I first met Donato Martinez over a decade ago at a professional development conference for college professors and counselors who worked for the Puente Project, a program designed to help Latino students transfer from junior college to a four-year university. It was the last day of the three-day conference and as was tradition at these gatherings, it was concluded with an open mic. After a few poets had gone up to the dais and read, the host spoke into the mic and called out the name Donato. From a chair at one of the tables I saw a large man slowly stand up. "Wow, this guy's tall," I recall quietly voicing to those around me, inciting a few laughs.

Although Donato's height can be intimidating, as soon as he speaks, you are put at ease. He has a calming voice and a tender nature. Quickly, you come to realize that the man is a gentle giant who speaks from the heart in language that is easy to understand. English peppered with Spanish. Formal dictum doused with slang. The vato was professional and cool. And instantly, I knew I was going to like both him and his written words. He did not disappoint.

Donato's poetry that afternoon was raw, relatable, rhythmic. I was easily captivated by the imagery and characters in his works. I could visualize scenes of the barrio where he grew up and feel a close connection to the people who called it home, from his close relatives to childhood friends. The Hip-Hop inspired rhythm of each poem, which kept the audience jiving with the poet the entire time, was also moving.

In this debut collection of poems, Donato continues to captivate and inspire. Recalling memories from childhood, he places us in the middle of the lives of a Mexican immigrant family attempting to carve out their little piece of the "American Dream." In one poem, he relates the story of his beloved mother, who "dropped out of school in the second grade," married at 16, and "immigrated to the United States with her family in 1973." However, as often happens with people who immigrate to this country from Mexico, work is prioritized over education. Left without a choice, they must work in order to survive and build a better future for their children. With this sentiment in mind, Donato continues this poem about his mother with what could have been had she "not been poor" or "raised in a pueblo." Expressing his affliction over what his mother has had to sacrifice for the benefit of her children and marriage to a man who "never flinched at hurting her," he writes, "With all that love, intelligence, and hustle, / This salt-of-the-earth woman, hecha de barro / May have been a teacher. Or an artist." What is certain to Donato, however, is that his mother "is the greatest storyteller."

Moving away from the nostalgic and melancholy, in another poem Donato navigates within the vein of the philosophical and political. Challenging Octavio Paz's views on the pachuco, the ultimate barrio hero, the poem opens with this stanza:

Creo en un solo vato
son of a pachuco zoot-suiter,
who threw down with the servicemen.
So, hey noble Nobel Prize Paz,
Give us peace.
Por favor.

This plea to the famed Mexican writer sets the stage for a greater view of the barrio where "vatos" and "jainas" embrace their identities while rejecting mainstream American society with all its discriminatory laws and propaganda created to keep brown people down. "I know who I am," Donato asserts, evoking the pachuco; and what follows is the unfolding of a tapestry decked in barrio images, from a Chicano youth "with a clean white, wife-beater / tucked into pleated khakis / and a paño around his forehead," to "vatos and jainas / cruis[ing] down the dark Boulevard on the '69 Impala." More than anything, the poem reads like an ode to the pachuco and the barrio that spawn him and his female counterpart, turning memories of oppression and struggle into beautiful sequences of a determined peoples' evolution. Coming full circle, the poem, however, turns back to the political with the following exclamation for a conclusion: "Fuck ICE."

As a seasoned professor of English and poetry connoisseur, in this book of his own poems, Donato pulls from his subject of expertise and from his own life experiences and creates a masterful work of art that is bound to break down "borders" and pave the way for other poets to come.

—Obed Silva, Professor of English, East LA College, author of *The Death of My Father the Pope*

Foreword
ANGELINA F. VEYNA

In a single collection of poems, Donato captures la gente de nuestras comunidades, and the kaleidoscope of everyday life activities, and the complexity of our emotions. He records the aspirations, the tristezas, las alegrias, the challenges, and the successes of our family members and friends. He pays homage to the hard work of our parents, and acknowledges the educación they gave us, yet, he is not afraid to also highlight the difficulties the new generations confront when there is a clash of beliefs and a difference in societal perspective. He acknowledges the homeland, Mexico, and explores the harrowing experiences of crossing the physical border, but also describes the many spiritual and cultural borders that must be confronted thereafter when adapting to a new society. He makes note of how long-held gender roles and expectations can affect and destroy the spirit of an individual.

Through his palabras, Donato presents and pays homage to the many men and women who often are excluded from our history books. He acknowledges their being, their presence, and the many contributions they make to our everyday life. Donato's poems make sure that we recognize their sudor, their hours of excessive work, and understand that they keep our cities in motion. Donato also describes the conditions of these lives; many of these trabajadores are forced to develop facades in order to hide the realities of poverty, discrimination, and second-class citizenship. Yet, nuestra gente is resilient, seguimos adelante, and develop a myriad of ways to survive and thrive in our barrios and colonias.

Donato also effectively captures the dynamism of everyday life and feelings. Through his choice of expressions and rhythm of words, he captures the multilingualism and multiculturalism present in our communities. He captures the kaleidoscope that we are and our cultura is. He captures the lives of the elders, of the new generations, of those who are in the netherworld of two lands, and the assimilated ones. As we read across the pages, his poetry provides soundtracks for us as he speaks of Marvin Gaye, of Chente Fernandez, or of Bob Marley. By the time we finish reading, Donato has us running to our local tiendita or restaurante because his description of enchiladas and mole just made us hungry.

He has continued the long-standing tradition of storytelling, and story-revealing that continues in our comunidades. Through Donato, la gente de nuestro pueblo y sus vidas están presentes!

—Angelina F. Veyna, Emeritus Professor of History, Santa Ana College

Foreword
DR. JESSICA AYO ALABI

Donato Martinez successfully gives us back the essence of poetic flow that's been missing from our lives during these uncertain times. His unique style, rhyme and cadence pull me back into the days of giving a damn, and living life freely, at the same time. Each metaphor serves to bring the reader into Martinez's world of cultura, familia, and comunidad that made him into who he is today. If you've never had days filled with wonderment, fear, laughter, and a sense of urgency all balled into one moment, do yourself a favor and float through his home-grown narration intentionally without pause.

He's undeniably Hip-Hop's offspring, which is evidenced by his inability to hide his love affair with musical genius. I found his writings to be a welcomed invasion of intimacy—touching upon topics that make us long for yesterday, yet race towards tomorrow. If you don't think about your own mother's sacrifice, perseverance, and candor after reading, "A Little Story About My Mother," you may have to read it again and again. Martinez's writings are an ode to the neighborhood, the homeboys, and the diverse gente that nurtured his precious love for storytelling. While the pain, the anger, and the prayers are soul-crushing and absorbed without interpretation, they steal nothing from his purity of heart on each page.

In "Sounds Ringing in My Ear," I could hardly maintain my composure while contemplating the struggle and heartache of good people in bad circumstances. Yet, Martinez reminds us, "We inhale, we exhale," and invites us to keep it pushing and don't give up. To truly embrace how Martinez captures the systemic problems of the likes of poverty, racism, miseducation, and outright exploitation, one must follow the low-riding messages hidden throughout his poems like the healing balm of an abuelo's orange in the face of what no child should ever have to experience.

Perhaps my favorite is, "Stupid Mexican, Sorry Ass American," because I know all too well what it's like to live in two worlds, code-switching your way to success, yet dying to keep it real. This piece only rivals, "Makes Me Wanna Holler," an homage to singer Marvin Gaye, but a delicate interrogation of masculinity from the vantage point of a man through a boy's eyes. Martinez has indeed given us our spoken word back in these lines that are wrapped up in his experiences, perceptions, and healing wounds.

—Dr. Jessica Ayo Alabi, Professor at Orange Coast College, Founder and CEO of Alabi Community Consulting

INTRODUCTION

I want to give a hug and a heartfelt thank you to anyone who has harbored any kind of faith and spirit in me. To the people that have pushed me to be a better person, professor, and poet; and to those that have nurtured my sense of exploration and wonder.

This collection of poetry is a long time coming. It is a tiny testament to things I have lived, experienced, seen, witnessed, heard. I am grateful for every single moment, good and bad. They are manifested in these poems. I harbor no ill will or resentment for anything. My sorrows, my pain, my frustration, my heartbreaks, my elation, my joy—they are all in here.

I have always been interested in people watching. Many times, when I was young, I was caught by the elders, as I eavesdropped in the kitchen or around grown men outside, always reprimanded and told to go play with my cousins. Even today as a grown person, my kids snap at me— "Apa, stop staring." Or some of my friends have nudged me disapprovingly, "Donato, you are such a bobo."

To the people that have stood by me, for a brief time or for years during times of doubt, failure, complacency. To those that were there for me during the toughest times in my life— you know who you are. I was in dark places, and you stood by me so I could see the light when my eyes refused to open. I wrote about these times with a relentless fever. Many of those notes and scribbles have found a home in this collection.

I am reminded by Notorious B.I.G. prologue on his classic song, "Juicy"—"Yeah, this album is dedicated to all the teachers that told me I'd never amount to nothin'. . ." If I could only return to my youth and teenage years and tell all the haters, "This is my story, and you are in it, because you tried to keep me down. And you humiliated my family. You spit in our path. You hurled obscenities." Even while I delivered newspapers early in the morning, or stocked the ice cooler with alcohol at a liquor store, or fried the chicken at Kentucky Fried Chicken, or cleaned the messes left by children at K-mart, I had plans beyond their expectations.

This collection is a celebration—of our past and present. It is about my family, our homes, our gente, our community, our language. It is about claiming a space, forcing to be recognized for the many contributions of our raza, on both sides of the border. It is about the beauty of our culture.

To those of you holding my book in your hands, Thank you so much from the bottom of my heart. You are celebrating my words. I hope you find yourself in one or two of these pieces. I hope you hear your voice in these. I hope you feel seen. I hope you feel understood. I hope you feel validated. Life is very beautiful. I hope you feel high. Let's touch the sky together.

With Love,

Donato Martinez

Donato, 6 years old at the Lincoln Elementary playground, Corona, California.

"How you gonna win/ if you ain't right within?"
—Ms. Lauryn Hill

"Joy, it's all founded / Pincher with the skin inside. . ."
—Bon Iver

"Don't you dare let our best memories bring you sorrow"
—Gregg Alexander

"I start to think, and then I sink / into the paper like I was ink/ When I'm writing, I'm trapped in between the lines / I escape when I finish the rhyme"
—Rakim

FEELS GOOD TO BE HOME

A Little Story About My Mother

My mother dropped out of school in the second grade.
She was raised in a pueblo and had little opportunities.
Despite the few years of school, she learned how to read and
      write in Spanish.
Learned mathematic equations
and taught her brothers how to write their names.

At 13 years old, she helped raised her cousin, whose mother
      died at childbirth.
At 16, she married my father.
And the little girl became a woman.
Quickly, she became a mother and raised her children on her
      own.
As my father worked in the yunta.
Every day she worried about what to feed them
and felt this pang of helplessness when they became sick.

During the summers she went to the nearby arroyo to wash
      baskets of clothes.
Other days she would haul cantaros full of water for meals and
      baths.
She would go to the molino for the masa on a daily basis.
Somehow, she was creative in making meals with the little she
      had.

She immigrated with her family in 1973
and her children enrolled at the local elementary school.
She never learned English
but picked up words enough to survive

when she helped make flour tortillas at her kids' schools.

She never had a job
except for a few scorching summers, picking grapes en los files
        de Fontana and Mira Loma
with her oldest children, she arrived before the crack of dawn.
By the midmorning sun, her cheeks became rosy red.
Her brows were smeared with dirt and sweat.
Her hair became untied and tangled underneath her hat
and the sand underneath her feet trampled her many times.
On the way home, she urged my oldest brother to drive
        quicker
for fear that her frijoles, slowly warming on the stove, would
        burn before she arrived.
My mother had her hustle.

When I was a little boy
late into the night, my mother would sneak into the bedrooms
of her children.
She made sure everyone was covered with a blanket
and whispered a tiny prayer in front of every sleeping child.

My mother was the victim of my father's anger.
She sustained many years of physical blows and verbal abuse.
He never flinched at hurting her
or hurling nasty obscenities in front of us screaming children.

She asked me about love one day. I tried to explain the feeling.
I told her I have felt it more than once.
She asked me to describe it. So, I did.
With sadness in her voice, she said,
"I have never known that feeling."

Now—I steal tiny moments as I come around the corner.
I watch her write in her tiny book of prayers.
I hear her oraciones to the Virgen de Guadalupe in the
           evenings.
Late into the night, I see her struggle to watch her novellas
           while she battles with her insomnia.

Like when I was a child, I still smell the canela on the stove,
the POND'S cream on her skin after an evening shower,
the spicy chile in a molcajete or the warm mole in the kitchen.

On most days now, she raises and cares and scolds my father
           as if he was her child.
And oftentimes, he is.

I often wonder what my mother's life would have been like
if she had not been poor, raised in a pueblo,
or married a man who didn't know how to love.

With all that love, intelligence, and hustle,
this salt of the earth woman, hecho de barro,
may have been a teacher. Or an artist.

However, she is the greatest storyteller.

Bendiciones de Cada Dia

Padre Nuestro,
que estás en el cielo o en los barrios,
danos hoy nuestro pan de cada día,
we'll take tortillas once in a while.
Pero, por favor oyeme Señor.

Y, perdona mis ofensas,
que if my jefita finds out
about the girl up the street,
me va a dar unos buenos chingadasos.

Please Dios, no me castigues
I can already hear my father,
        "Pasguato, hasta rebotas de tan pendejo."

Dolores, como la pinche joda
on 5 a.m. summer grape-picking days
en los files de Mira Loma y Fontana:
        "Huevones, ya levantense
        que vamos a la friega,
        agarren sus tacos de huevos y papas,
        que ya se va el Toro Mascado."

        "Y, be careful crossing the railroad tracks,
        hang on to the door handle,
        the gears slip every once in a while,
        pero no te preocupes,
        que el claxon si jala rete bien."

Riding the banana-colored school buses to school
carrying a Don Leon Tortilla bag, knotted and braided,
keeping tacos de frijoles Reynolds Wrap-ped warm until lunch
with an orange,
and a smeared peanut butter and jelly *sanwish*
hidden under the seat, between scaly feet.

> "Y, mijo, no seas tan malvado
> y, don't look at that filthy chucho up the street taking a
>   shit,
> porque se te van a salir granos en los ojos.
> Y, mija, pon cuidado en la school,
> pero dile al pinche Mr. Smith to take his hands off your
>   skirt,
> que ya sabe tu papa.
> Y, no te juntes con esos cholillos.
> Porque if I find out, te voy a dar una buena bofetada,
> y, ustedes muchachos ya charapense,
> y, venganse a comer,
> y, no sean tan malcriados,
> o les va un buen wammazo en su hosiko.
> Y, don't give me that look, porque asi se les van a
>   quedar sus caras,
>   cabrones esquinkles."

And during the cool evenings,
playing canicas on the dirt driveways
dodging cars up and down the street while smacking baseballs
watching young girls hopscotching or mecatiando in the
            middle of the street.

Days like Saturday morning Hilguerillas,

Lucha Villa,
or old Vicente Fernandez,
on muffled record players or old 8-track cassette players
and the smell of Pine-Sol or Fabuloso.
Cus today is cleaning day.

Y despues, vamos de salida
and riding through town
in the two-door, '68 green-chipped roof Impala.

Afternoon in the cafeteria
slurping Slurpees
gobbling greased, buttered popcorn,
waiting for the K-mart Blue Light Specials.
Okay muchachos, now we can start shopping,
        "No, ya les dije, put those Hot Wheels back.
        No Converse today, only get the Zips or the Keds."
Stops at Zody's, Gaines, and TG&Y
rematiando y regateando.
Packed like sardines in one car to drive-in theaters.

Sounds of a Mexican home:
gasnuchos
chanclasos,
huarachasos,
y fajerasos for muchachos mal educados,
papalote,
chocolate,
zopilote,
cacahuates,
that remind us of our indigenous roots
chicharrones,

chilaquiles,
burros de sal y mantequilla
on pockedmarked flour tortillas
fresh off the smoked, Oaxacan comal,
the roasted, toasted green chiles on ancient stone molcajetes
        become the best salsa verde
like agaucates become Chicano become guacamole,
or sucking on chile saladitos in the middle of a limon wedge
in the parking lots of local liquor stores.

Savoring the charcoaled burnt edges of abuelita's gorditas de
        horno,
Salivating over mole, atole, y pozole
Nothing like a bowl of menudo after a buena cruda, Ask your
        tio.

Remedios caseros
de yerba buena,
te de limon,
cotton balls on sunken bellybuttons,
foreheads wrapped in alcohol and marijuana-drenched rags,
scratches and gashes ointed with savila
burns and rashes smeared with mayonnaise or toothpaste
smeared juice and tomato seeds on balding hair,
toasted lemon halves on itching mosquito bites,
gulping Sal de Uvas for nauseous stomachs,
and swallowing smeared Vapor-Rubbed fingers.

A buena sobada
or a curada from the curandera
with the crooked foot and blind left eye.

"Y muchacho malvado
mas te vale que vayas a misa
a confesarte,
o te va a castigar Dios."

I Come From Dirt

—to my siblings, you are the flowers that grew from dirt

I come from dirt.
      I come from dirt
and from the scorching sun on the back of my father and the
      sweaty brow of my mother.

I come from adobe homes with an array of chickens, dogs,
      and cows in the backyard.
From fences made of neatly-stacked boulders and rocks.

I come from a place of beautiful dreams, but rarely fulfilled,
just hung up on some clothesline along some white, washed
      sheets.

I come from where the church bells ring every hour.
And remind us of prayers and faith on early Sunday mornings.

I come from the long black hair of mothers kneeling in a pew
and the black veil that hides their tears of sadness
who lose children to sickness, accidental death, or revenge-
      killing.

From young women who know no love, marry without love.
And birth children whom they deeply love.

I come from a place of sorrow and misery.
A place of broken hearts and shattered promises
A place of wounded spirits.

I come from snotty-nosed children going hungry.
And leaving school to help their family.
Children whose clothes are begged, borrowed, or stolen.

Children who immigrate with their families
and are left alone in homes
waiting for mothers and fathers to return home after 12 hours
        of work.
Children who read mail, translate at doctors' appointments,
        and school meetings in their own broken language,
who have forgotten their Spanish and who have not fully
        embraced their English.

I come from dirt.
But from this place rises the beautiful earthy, orange clay that
        gives birth to hopes and dreams.
A place of humility and hard work and resiliency
of chile, nopales and maiz tortillas warming on the hot comal
of hot chocolate brewing on the stove keeping us warm on
        cold days.

I come from men who tilled the soil and harvested their own
        crops.
And fed 100 people with seven corn, five potatoes, and three
        squash.
These same men who fought off mountain lions with
        huaraches while crossing the border.

I come from the powerful eyes of women
of silent strength
of women who dance on top of clouds
and who learned the secret healing power of herbs

these same women that learned the language of love
and speak with the moon and stars and other galaxies
who summon the rains to come with trembling power.

I come from the amazing colors of the rainbows
from the fiery setting sun that unleashes its last rays
before it succumbs
to the purple beauty of the night sky
          that breathes life
                    and hope
                        into those of us
                            who come from dirt.

Oranges at My Grandfather's

—to my Papa Donato

I used to watch my grandfather pull out a pocketknife from
        his pocket.
He'd find an orange
and slice it into perfect wedges right on the palm of his hand.
It was a ritual, like making magic out of nothing.

These were our summers when we were out of school.
It was our escape.
Our vacation—just walk up the street and I would be at his
        home.

My cousins and I would salivate and drool over the oranges.
The sticky and juicy mess would run down from our fingertips
        to our elbows
and we wiped our hands on our shirts
only to stain them with permanent smudges
        and ask him for more.

It was these summers
that reminded us of our innocence
as we bravely escaped and got lost in the jungle of gardens and
        plants and vegetables.
We created backyard adventures as we climbed apricot trees.
We discovered the mystery and nudity of women in old
        Playboy magazines.
Some of us learned about the bitter taste of alcohol.
And the stale stench of cigarettes.

Like scavengers we quickly ran to our homes with glee
        out of breath.
And for a night, we forgot about our sadness
and hid the grief of our own homes.
The scars of our past.
The sins of our fathers.
Of fights and hunger and poverty and screams.
And promised not to share the dark family secrets that destroy
        families.

        One day things will get better. I promise you.
        We nodded in agreement.

And we will remember:

How my grandfather wounded an orange so perfectly
And how quickly we devoured the sweet flesh.

My Mother, the Sculptor

—a mi madre

From the crack of the door
the early morning smell
of fresh tortillas,
and the sound of music
from the slap of her hands,
awaken my soul
and enter the palate of my mente.

Jefita's rebozo cradles her back
warms her innocent neck.
Her fingers sticky with masa,
forming, shaping, embracing it
into small balls of dough.

Hot coffee brewing on the stove.
Likes it hot.
Adds milk and a spoon of sugar.
Dips into it with a piece of soft bolillo
before French rolls, bagels, or croissants
came to America.

Her hands are forming tiny little miracles.
Grows yerba buena,
bathes her infants in magical mirto.
Roasts red chiles on a Oaxacan comal
crushes tomatillos on sacred Molcajetes.
Dices onions,

slices tomatoes.

Michelangelo and Rodin
would have learned a thing or two
from my Indian mother,
who loves the moods of the land,
works and toils the soft soil
with her pineapple-callused hands.
Small fingers,
cut and scratched by tunas and nopales,
pricked by rose bushes.

Her mandil,
old and tattered from years of toil.
And every smear, smudge and stain tells a story
　　　of how my mother came to be a sculptor.

Hispanic Graduation U.S.A.

10-dollar entrance fee,
for a chile relleno dinner
and a side of Rosarita beans,
with a sprinkle of sharp cheddar cheese,
and flan for dessert.

Everyone is properly dressed,
well-groomed,
lathered-up
gelled-up
firmly-fitting in those
navy blue and gray,
double-breasted suits,
long-sleeved, oxford shirts
silk ties,
wing-tip shoes.

And they all look so good,
in their upward mobility
glasses . . .
and cellphones.

Tonight, they will recognize this year's Hispanic Graduates,
as the keynote warns of
inflation, poverty, and other social ills that await them
while promoting mainstream participation
and economic power,
but warning those who forget one's roots.

Several men shyly look away,
as they pass out business cards,
and the keynote speaker makes no sense.
But he specializes in International Relations and Business
        Marketing.
He must know a thing or two about a thing or two.

And as we stand in line for food,
while others mingle about
good books they plan to read
and vacations they plan for this summer,
I notice my father's attire.

Underdressed, maybe not even appropriate for this occasion.
His hair is a bit uncombed,
and has a tiny leaf in it.
He wears brown socks
with those shabby and scuffed-looking black shoes
that he gardens, shops, and goes to church in.
He has a firme looking, black and blue-checkered flannel shirt
        on
that many vatos locos would admire.

But I doubt they would tuck it in like my father does
into a pair of gray corduroy pants,
        smeared with dirt on the pockets,
sagging way below his waistline.
He coordinates these pants
with an outdated, white, fake snakeskin belt.
He probably has a couple jalapeños
or some fresh cheese in his pocket.

And I realize that no fashion designer
has ever seen such a thing.
It could become a trend though.

After being recognized and saying a few words,
I return to my seat
where my parents
and brother are waiting.
I hand my father my graduate certificate
printed by a laser writer,
and he says the most profound thing of the whole night:
"Tanto pinche tiempo de estudio, para este papelito."

And in that moment, I realize
that it is good to be alive
because being seated next to my father,
reminds me that even in a congregation of Hispanics,
it's still possible to be a real Mexican.

Mestizo Picadillo

Mestizo beats
on underground airwaves
      samplin' 'n scratchin'
            mixing and minglin'
                  blendin' 'n bendin'
                        borrowin' and takin.'

Lyrical passwords
breaking the rusted chains of slavery
and waking decaying
skeletons, skulls, and bones
running through clay earth
      and creepin' through time
            ticking and tocking
to packs of wolfs
and ancient sacred spirits
      hummin'
           crumblin,'
                rumblin,'
                    'n tumbling.'

Tribal Tenochtitlan temples.
Live hearts oozin' 'n drippin'
      warm sacrificial blood
just spreadin' n' descending
past descendants of Machu Picchu
with ceremonial, Calypso and Conga drums,
      thump
           thump

thumping.

Inca Flutes,
Aztec conch shells
solo-strummin' acoustic guitars
and bass-infused Caribbean beats
        slidin'
                and electric bugalooing
birthin' births and deaths
        and rebirths.

To Pan-Africans
mulattos
sambos
and Indians.
Mestizo schoolchildren
and Creole teachers
are scratchin' and scrawling on chalkboards
rewriting and recreating history
not HIS story,
our story, and checkin' it
        check,
                check,
                        checkin' it.

Cacophonous hieroglyphic rhythmic
beebops and Hip-Hops
rattling rattles, maracas, and timbales
carving and etching cherubed flesh
slicing and slippin' infant ear drums.

Strange Voodoo sounds

Voodoo sounds
and Ho-Ho's
shrieking curses and chanting
        speaking in tongues
and smoking peace pipes and slowly burning incense.

Evenings of surreal dreams and late-night screams
scandalous vibrations
and pelvic gyrations
whispering sweet and charming incantations
in between moist blankets
of midnight, snake-wrapped lovers.

Just for the funk of it,
ferociously
grooving 'n freakin'
shakin' 'n bakin'
jammin' 'n jivin'.

Secretly and discreetly
scribbling our heart
                beats
on dark corners of our virgin, sacred land
that Columbus has not yet tainted.

Speaking in Tongues

"Wild tongues can't be tamed, they can only be cut out."
—Gloria Anzaldúa

My native tongue curls around
trying to find space for a new language in my mouth.
I stumble across metaphors and similes while my Nahuatl
     vernacular
hangs on to my Spanish-speaking pueblo.

This new language imprisons
my ancestor's survival
but I'm a she and a he
dark and white
a mestizo picadillo
so, I invent a language
a tongue that is wicked and strange.

Crunchy cacahuate shells are strewn on dirt driveways
muchachas hauraches hopscotch on white chalk squares on
     sidewalk-less streets
orale vatos locos crouch old school style
with sips of secret drinks inside paper sacks
dropping liquor and street wisdom to young schoolboys
Aztec grandmothers pass down recipes of tamales and mole
     and nopales
as gifts to Mexicana mothers
hovering over pots of brewing frijoles
turning and rotating home-made maiz tortillas

and burning fingers on hot comales
chavalos y mocosillos make burritos de sal y mantequilla.

Mothers sew and stitch old sweaters into place,
iron patch on holey knees of Levi's pants handed down from
    older brothers
clean bruised knees and scraped elbows of mijito's fall from
    his bicycle
spitshine their children's hair and spit-wipe their milk
    mustaches before rides on the school bus
grandfathers slice oranges with red pocketknives while
    storytelling
about el terre and arboles and arroyos being chingones
y caballos bien finos
they complain about pinches tios borachos, buenos pa nada, ni
    valen setenta chingadas
about el pinche gallo que no me dejaba dormir.

They retell stories
about mujeres bien preciosas cuando era joven
about the time, "Que perdi mi primavera in the back of the
    church right next to the old viejita's house."

These oral tales are strung together
weave the past, present, and future together
in cyclical time
the hot sun disappears
into a lovely evening of purple serenata colors
and the guitar strings serenade la viuda joven
que matarron a su esposo en El Norte
where the blazing sun rises and shines early on piscadores'
    backs

piscando fruta en los files de Delano y Mira Loma.

The same night when the pinche chota pulled me over
porque me vio muy esquinkle
y me dio un tiquete porque
I didn't stop over the railroad tracks
because my jefe's troca esta bien vieja and the brecas ni sirven
        para nada.

Grandmothers weep in heavy breaths
their long life of curing fevers, sarampion, y birguelas
with their magical curandera hands
they slice their own varicose veins
con el mismo cuchillo que cortan cebollas
collect the blood in tin cups
finger rosaries
offer prayer after prayer for la Virgen Maria, Tonantzin
pa que se alivie su hermano de cancer
so, his nephew crosses the migra checkpoint safely
pa que le den trabajo
y pa que le mande dinero a su vieja que esta embarasada.

This Chicano tongue is more complex than French kissing for
        the first time
as I stumble on sloppy saliva
trying to fit these new words in my mouth
of forced Spanish, bien chueco y mocho, the grade-school
        learned English, barrio street vernacular, pocho talk,
        and bits and pieces of slang and talking shit.

I speak in tongues
this tongue is a gift that is wicked and strange.

I create it.

And I don't need to apologize.
And I am sick of translating.

Stupid Mexican, Sorry-Ass American

"He who serves two masters, disappoints one . . . or both"
—Jose Burciaga

I live in the borderlands too.
I am not Mexican enough. Americans think I have too much
      barrio in me.

I love grilled hot dog wieners wrapped inside a tortilla.
I prefer carne asada and frijoles during 4th of July.
But I love pizza more than caldo de rez.

Street tacos with guacamole salsa is delicious anytime.
So are double doubles from In-N-Out especially after a night
      of drinking.

I only eat nopales with a mediocre interest, much like
      cauliflower.
Mexican pan dulce is overrated.
I don't eat capirotada.

I ask for salsa or chiles at American diners.
My father has even walked into Denny's with fresh queso and
      tortillas in his back pocket.

I love baseball and basketball with a passion
but I take little interest in soccer.
I bump Hip-Hop more than Norteño music.
I even like The Smiths more than Chente.

I am such a bad Mexican.

My mother tongue has lost its grip on me
cus I get confused with translating words like embarrassed
        with embarazada.
Or support and no te soporto.
I just learned that a gall bladder is vesicula or is it bicicleta?
When I was younger, I had trouble translating letters for my
        parents.
Even at appointments, my father berated me for not
        understanding doctors.

When I get pissed, I shout in Spanish—"¡Pinche Pendejo!"
The most offensive curse words in Spanish begin with the
letter "P."
Growing up, my white friends always asked me to teach them
        curse words in Spanish.

When I see a friend from a distance, White or Mexican,
        I nod in the Mexican, male gesture of recognition.

I learned the Padre Nuestro as a child and still recite it at night
        especially after bad dreams
but I feel a sense of conflict and guilt over reciting the Pledge
        of Allegiance
or standing for the National Anthem.

I love America, but America does not always love me.
I don't trust the police, but I detest ICE. Pinches vendidos.

I am the son of Mexico. But the USA has adopted me.

Spanish was my first tongue; There is no translation for,
      "Te amo."
I teach English. Sometimes my accent is very apparent.
I fell in love with writing by reading literature written in
      English.

I am such a horrible Mexican. I am an even a worse American.
Mejicanos call me pocho. My Chicano friends say I am too
      paisa sometimes.
I censor my speech among Whites.

I am caught between two worlds. Not knowing which one to
      call home.
I am a stranger in my own land. Even more so in Mexico.

I am a stupid Mexican. A sorry-ass American.

Make a Run for the Border

Make a run for the border.
Leave the firing squads and bloody civil wars.
Leave the communists, dictatorships, and "perfect
        democracies" behind.
There will be no more kidnapped journalists and imprisoned
        poets.
Leave the poverty, dirty streets and cobblestone roads, and
        stale bread.
Leave the high unemployment rates.
Leave the Aztec ruins in ruin.

Make a run for the border.
Hurry, here's your last chance.
The gates are flooded open.
The barbwire has been cut loose.
America is selling plenty of dreams.
And the Statue of Liberty is embracing you with welcome
        hugs.

What you waiting for?
Disneyland has sale and clearance items.
The Electrical Parade is a nightly event.
Mickey Mouse is finished with Minnie
and he's looking for another hood rat, a new squeeze.
McDonald's is open 24 hrs. with a friendly smile.
Get your French fries while they're hot.

Haven't you heard?
Money falls from trees.

Collect it in bundles and sacks.
Buy beautiful 2 car garage homes
with green manicured lawns and friendly neighbors nearby
white picket fences and poodle dogs
sprinklers, newspapers, bagels, and coffee every morning.

They're selling
Botox
liposuction
and Victoria's Secret on the internet.
Anybody can be beautiful.

Make a run for the border.
You will have no need to shop at swap meets
browse through junk
at garage and yard sales
or collect aluminum cans in hefty black Glad bags
or wait in lines for handouts at food co-ops at homeless
       shelters.
No more fried manteca,
Chicharron, or burnt tire smells.

Make a run for the border.
Hurry. You won't ever have to pick oranges or grapes
or fill them in wood crates for 25 cents
wash dirty sheets from strangers' sex
scrub food and ketchup smears off dishes.
You will never have to cut or manicure another lawn other
than your own.
No more digging ditches
or hustling for jobs at Home Depot with other compas.

Make a run for the border before you get trapped
in housing projects
into receiving welfare checks
        and Government cheese.
No more licking stamps on booklets
making powdered Tang and Kool Aid.
Oh Yeah!

Hurry, make a run for the border.
Run as fast as you can north on the 5 freeway, across six lanes
in front of screeching tires and sirens in the night light.
Hold your children and your lifelong belongings as tightly as
        you can.

Don't get pulled over or harassed by police or ICE officials.
They will baton whip you
into a lifeless mass of blood and guts.
They won't ask questions or care about your name.

Hurry. Make a run for the border.
Watch your back
or you'll get 3 tons of concrete rubble shoved up your ass
or barbed wire tangled around your bleeding emotional
        sensitive heart
split between your legs
gouge and rip the flesh off your flesh
the blood off your blood.
This body that is shed for America.
Rack your body
year after year
of this cycle of poverty
this cycle that you succumb to

this cycle that you sacrifice to.

So, hurry and make a run for the border
What you waiting for?
And keep your head up.

* The title "Make a Run for the Border" taken from Taco
Bell's 1988 commercial, *Make a Run for the Border*

In Case You Don't Feel Hip-Hop

I want mad crazy hops
like brothers who cross you over on basketball blacktops
they walk, swagger, and rhythm in their crazy wild socks
ghetto blasters nearby bumping loud Hip-Hop
that rattle and shake the windows on your block
it's never too early to make your body pop n' lock
sizzle and flame on your tongue like pop rocks
words that rhyme, spitting and spraying a beatbox
perfect circles like Cheerios in a cereal box
Kindergarten children collecting box tops
and special surprises inside the Cracker Jack box.

Young brothers boppin' heads
hair like moppy dreadlocks
Bob Marley resurrects on corner blocks
old school jams are playing on the jukebox
in a pool hall with sexy females that make your body rock.

Yo—I'm talking about Hip-Hop
at times it's about the fashion
but it's always deeper like passion.

Listen to Hip-Hop
and drop some sad tears
shots of hard liquor or spill a cold beer
for the homie from the early school years.

Some rappers give us a hit and quickly disappear
but real artists have been around for more than 20 years.

Some Hip-Hop artists are already dead
but you can't get their music out of your head
you recite their lyrics while lying in bed
love songs are nice, but I want Hip-Hop instead.

Delicious like mother's good food
cozy, like a breezy afternoon
or happy
   like holding hands and feeling so good
   or skipping rope in a chipper, good mood.

Hip-Hop can be nice and chill
   like the deep cherry moon.
You fall asleep
   grooving and humming that tune.

The music sounds so good, it picks you right up
like nodding your head and saying, "What's up?"

Hip-Hop makes you scream,
but inspires you to dream.

It can bring you hope
when you're feeling alone.

Music hits you hard
thrusts you in the heart
deep feelings like art
it can make you soar and fly far
   like a comic book superstar
or shine like a falling bright star.

Makes you feel love
for the very first time.
Nervous sweet lines.
She's a poem that rhymes.

You gotta believe
      just one time to listen.
I'm sure you will see.
It helps me feel free
shines bright for me
like high beams in front of me
that help me to see   clearly.

You see—
Hip-Hop lets me be.

And
Yo—
I just want to BE.

It's a Funky World

Oral tales
going way back into legendary time
of funkmaster heroes
spreading hereditary funk
funk lore
of funky gods and goddesses
and funky myths.

Soul Train funky rhythms
of fevered funkadelic nights
of early 80's old school funk
after the strobe light dog days and nights of disco deejays
        and Bebop wops.

That funky groove
it's funk-o-matic
doing the funky chicken
        the Kentucky Fried Chicken
                finger-licking it,
funky delicious
funk dubious
        the doobiest
the grooviest.

Little funky beats
and all that scratching is making me itch,
won't Hang the DJ
        if he plays that funky music white boy.

Doing the mo' better funky
        the nasty,
                the freak.
With funky moves,
funky pelvic gyrations
trying to get the funky jiggy on,
like Dr. Funkenstein
        funking this
                funking that.

Everybody's got the funk
everybody's doing the funk
        Just for the funk of it
        one nation under a funky jam.

May the funk be with you
and whatever you do it's got to be funky,
cus it's a funky world,
and you got to funk
or be funked.

Santa Maria

—inspired by the image and life of Maria Sabina, curandera and poet

MARIA
MARIA
MARIA

firewalker
spiritwalker
shaman
curandera
healer
poet-singer-dancer
Mazatec woman, Oaxacan sage
bring down your spirit and your vision
to bring the sacred to the profane
to cleanse this world
and elevate my soul

Santa Maria
God is jealous of your power
and men are threatened by your magic
mothers come to you with children sick since birth
old men cripple their way to you
and women betrayed by love
with infants in their arms
come to you to mend their broken hearts
your soul rises and enters
into the sparkle of their eyes

MARIA
MARIA
MARIA

poets, artists, and musicians seek your spiritual truth
and your deep ceremonial healing
to see the clear vision in their own eyes
to dream again
breathe life and fire in their own work
with passion, fury, and vengeance
they find new truth in their soul
because of you

yes, you
you helped shape a world that is beautiful
and now magic rises from the voice of the poet
from the strings of the musician's guitar
from the sunrise colors of the palette
that bleeds crimson red from the artist's canvas down to the
        floor
keeper of faith
keeper of indigenous secrets
mother earth
that roamed the clay earth
brown magic woman, hecho de barro
of long and lonely walks en las calles
                        en los files
                        en el barrio

MARIA
MARIA
MARIA

let me hear your rhythmic chant
your whistle, hum, song, and clap
let me honor you with a poem or a song
or in a dance in a trance that lasts all night long
I want to see the clashing of the stars
the kaleidoscope of geometric shapes and rich colors
architectural structures that rise to the sky
I want to experience the epiphany of visionaries
of root doctors
shamans and saints
I want to rise like a flower to sky
to bring truth and purify my life

should I share your name
in a whisper or a scream?
with a tear or a long howling wail?
with one line or in a long epic poem
in a prayer or a song?
Santa Maria
Santa Sabina

you suffered for sharing the secrets
of the little magical mushrooms
I too weep and wail over the tragedies and maladies of your
        life
the burning of your house
and the murder of your son

let me glance upon you one more time
at the gold bronze that gleams from your perfect saintly face
your wrinkled, scarred, hands

permanently etch the lifelines of struggles and tragedy
and the many wars you fought and survived
wave goodbye to me one final time
let the speckles of gold dust rise from your hands
to protect me from the evil spirits that trek the earth

and I shall call you by your name
Santa Maria
Maria Sabina

and I will call and I will sing and I will chant and I will hum
        and I will wail
and I will scream and I will howl and I will write the ceremony
        of your name:

MARIA
MARIA
MARIA

To My Daughter

You are God's presence
      in my presence.
I cherish this tiny moment.
                         Now.
Because you are the present.

You are the glistening stars on my back.
The bright moon light in the celestial night sky.
You are the goosebump chills on my skin.
You are the gold dust speckles that rise from the palm of my
      hands.
The warm blood that runs deep in my veins.
You are the natural wonders of my being.
      You are my being . . . completely.
And I am whole because you complete me.

You are the colors that flutter and butterfly my insides
the chilly cool water that flows down rivers and streams.
You are the hunger of life
the dream of a new tomorrow
      the inspiration of a sad day.

And if I followed the rainbow
I would see you next to it reading a book.

You are my epiphany
my spiritual guide
the wings on my back
that help me float among the cotton candy clouds.

You are the sunrise and sunset of every day.

You are the truth that is in the innocence of your eyes.

You protect me and elevate me.
You are my hope to my future
one with tranquil evenings
and peaceful melancholic sunsets.
You are my beginning and end.
You are the comfort of my rest.
You are the streaks of sunlight across a gray, lazy morning.

You are the glue to my fractured mess
the stitch that mends my wounds
the eraser that forgives my sins.
You are the healing to my scars.
You are the sad puffy eyes of innocence and truth.

You are my third eye wisdom and my vision.
My sixth sense and my secret intuition.
You are the language of my hopes and dreams
and you take me to a higher plane.

You are eternal
the bluest of the flame
the spirit
the forever.

And I feel your essence.
You are his presence.
Cus you are the present.

Now.

At this moment.

And I will cherish this tiny moment.

When Gabriel Was Small

When Gabriel was small, he pleaded for another story, for ten more minutes. He bartered and bartered for more time. Later, he stole more minutes as he sneaked books between his sheets at night. With a night-light flickering on and off, he read whole sentences, whole paragraphs, even whole chapters. Before the cocks crowed in the morning and even before the new sunlight, with sleepy eyes, he read new letters and new words. He was mesmerized. He read about wild animals, dinosaurs, dragons, planets, and stars. He thought about complex questions that have no answers.

He left his parents very young, and as the years passed Gabriel traveled very far to visit distant places and meet new people. He fought with evil knights and fire-breathing dragons. He was enchanted by the mystery of wizards, the African lions in the middle of the hunt in the heat of the Serengeti. He sang choruses with the birds in the tropical rain forests. He witnessed meteors that reshaped the world, and women that danced on top of clouds. He trekked and scaled large, rocky, mountains. He perched himself on top of pyramids and flung himself across the beauty of the night sky to celestial planets in search of his origins.

Gabriel has walked and traveled very far, to many strange places. But, he was never alone. He was always accompanied by the call of his new friends, by the echoes of the canyons, by the music and sound of birds, the whisper of a breeze, and by the laughter of children. These peaceful sounds kept him company. In fact, Gabriel is not the same anymore.

These places, people, and mythical creatures are so much a part of him, that now they live inside him. And he is never alone.

For My Daughter, if You Ever Need Me

Tupac rapped, "And since we all came from a woman
Got our name from a woman and our game from a woman
I wonder why we take from our women
Why we rape our women, do we hate our women?
I think it's time to kill for our women
I think it's time to heal our women, be real to our women."

So, mija. Let me be real to you:
If you ever need me, I am here for you.
If a man wounds your spirit
and takes the sweet honey from your tender heart,
      I won't pretend that it will never happen again.
If a man disrespects you, I am sorry that it may not be the last
      time.
If a man takes what's yours without asking
or if he humiliates you in public, I will not hesitate to
      relinquish my pent-up wrath
and regulate my fury upon his face.

If you need to confide in me, I will listen attentively and with
      compassion.
I will reciprocate with honesty and sensitivity.
I will comfort you when you are sad and heartbroken.

Mija. Men are pigs and dogs.
You will confront
unwanted comments and invitations
catcalling
whistling

sexual gestures
gawks and uncomfortable stares.

You will also confront hate from evangelical prophets
only interested in making profits.
These same men who bullshit and twist biblical verses
so that you and your best friends seek underground
            black-market relief
With strangers' hands and hangers twisting inside you
while you writhe in pain and fear.

These same men that pass laws against your gender.
No man. No law. No policy. No gun
can tell you what to do with your body. Ever.

You must always choose You.

You are a daughter of the earth. A daughter born of love. A
            daughter born of fire.
A daughter born of all that is natural. You are a daughter of
            wisdom and courage.

There is marrow and blood that courses in your body
from sacred, mother earth,
from all the female sages and visionaries.
You are a daughter of shamans and medicine women. That
            chose you.

So, you choose you.

Just one more thing:
Stay away

from fuckboys
And douchebags
And drunk and slobbering fools.

Just a man that is equal to you.
One that shields you.
One that protects you.
One that walks beside you, not in front of you.

One that holds your heart in the tenderness of his palm
but kindly releases you when you want to be let go
like the wounded bird ready to flee
like the relentless and independent spirit that you are.

Mija. Always choose YOU.
You are Resiliency. Love. Courage. Wisdom.

TOUGH LOVE

We Wanted More

We wanted more. We always wanted more.
All seven of us.

We were hungry. We wanted more than wrapped burritos and oranges for lunch. We wanted more than frijoles and tortillas. We wanted more than caldo. We wanted to eat at restaurants. We wanted McDonald's. We wanted Kentucky Fried Chicken.

We wanted more treats. We wanted ice cream. I would sneak Doritos bags underneath the sandwich bread. Ding Dongs under the bananas. I would replace Corn Flakes with Frosted Flakes. I stole snickers bars and bags of M&M's.

We wanted longer showers. More time with warm water. More time in the bathroom. We wanted our own room. Our own bed. Our own blanket. But we shared everything. Clothes. Jackets. Shoes. Combs. Sandals. One television.

We wanted to get away. We wanted to move. We wanted a bigger home. With a large backyard. And a tiny playground. We wanted to smell fresh flowers. Not chicken smells. Or burnt rubber smells. Or littered car part smells. Or dog smells. We wanted fresh lemonade in the refrigerator.

We wanted a nice haircut at a barber shop. Not one from Pops. He fucked up our hair every time.

We wanted Nike shoes. Or Adidas. Or Vans. We got Keds. Or other knockoff generic brands bought at Kmart or the swap meet.

We wanted a new bike for all of us. I didn't mind if we shared this. With handbrakes. Or multiple gears. Because our cousin had a new one. He didn't share with anyone. We wanted a new car during high school. Because he had one.

We wanted vacations and trips to the beach. We wanted to go camping. We wanted to sleep underneath the stars. We wanted to go to the mountains. We wanted to go fishing. Because other boys in our classes did that.

We wanted Santa Claus to visit our home. We wanted a Christmas tree full of presents. We wanted birthday parties. We wanted birthday cakes with candles. We wanted to spend the night at friends' homes. We wanted more. We always wanted more.

He spanked our tiny asses. Sometimes with his bare hands. Often with his leather belt. Red, raw marks. The pain was like gas poured on fire. The pain spread across our backs and up our necks. The back of our thighs bubbled with red welts.

He whipped us across our round butts. For playing outside. For not pulling weeds. For talking during dinner. For coming home after dark. For bickering with each other over an Atari game. We wanted our mother when he screamed and knocked us down with a stinging slap to our heads. We wanted her to comfort us.

We wanted good times with him. We wanted laughter. We wanted him to throw the ball with us. We wanted swings in the back yard. We wanted to crawl up his legs and sit on his lap. We wanted and craved hugs from him. The affection never came.

We wanted more. We always wanted more.

All seven of us.

Where I'm From

—to the barrio, Home Gardens

Where I'm from—the front porch is an extension of the living room. Where my white friend first learned of tamales. You must unwrap the cornhusk before biting into the creamy, chile-filled masa.

I'd sit for hours spitting sunflower seeds and contemplating the beautiful girl from my class I was too afraid to talk to.

Where I'm from, I'd peel oranges while doing my algebra homework while I waited for my mother's mole.

On any given day, music blasted from the inside. The thumping loud sounds would shake and rattle screen doors that were held together by one screw on its side. The music was tropical and funky. The Hip-Hop beats were loud and bombastic. Classic times of whole afternoons as I became entranced to the glorious spells of music. It was one of my first loves.

Where I'm from the sirens kept us up all night—from police cars, ambulances, and fire trucks. Even helicopters circled around the night sky beaming and shining its high beams across the asphalt streets.

Where I'm from German shepherds and rottweilers and cock-fighting roosters competed for attention with the borachos and tecatos who stumbled home drunk or high in the early morning hours. Shortly thereafter a young mother would plead, "No viejo, it wasn't me. It's not true. Stop screaming. You're gonna wake up the kids. Please Dios, por favor. Ayudame."

"Shut the fuck up you fucken' puta. Antes que te quebre el hosico."

Where I'm from the smells of family creeps out of every opening, pore, crack, hole, and spills into the air like confetti. It is the warm pot of frijoles, handmade corn tortillas hot off the comal, toasted green chiles peeled and crushed into a smoky molcajete.

Where I'm from the blaring sounds of horns, music, children, ice cream trucks keep everyone awake and alert.

Cars litter driveways, yards, and large patches of dirt. All are works in progress.

Empty beer cans are scattered all over the front yard like permanent decorations. Marijuana smoke penetrates nostrils.

Young children play hopscotch in the middle of the street as they dodge low-riders cruising slow and low to the sounds of oldies.

Where I'm from concrete walls are never bare—inscriptions are scrawled. Barely legible graffiti claims a clica or a barrio. Names of lovers are etched out and painted over by young novice muralists. Hearts are glorified. Suns and moons are painted. And rainbows provide colors to the drab streets. These walls leave memories of who was here.

Where I'm from fresh grasses sprout.
Fruit trees grow wildly like a jungle in the backyard.
Wildflowers push through cracks in the concrete.
Shaky hands of grandmothers tend immaculate rosebush
       gardens.
Young girls jump rope in the middle of the street.
Teenage boys toss baseballs and make plans to become boxers
       or ballers.

Where I'm from . . . through the crumbled cinderblocks, between cracked cement, and potholes on asphalt streets, tell a future of innocent shortys that read books and become lawyers and teachers.

Where I'm from—it is still possible to make dreams come true. It is possible to make a mother smile and to make your sister cry tears of joy.

Hood Stories

Nahuatl palabras beautifying the antepasados and giving tribute to our ancestral roots. Like papalotes and tecolotes. Aguacates become Chicano become guacamole. Because we are keeping the language alive. With greetings of our beautiful gente. And, "Mexica Tiahui hermano." Y, "Buenos dias compadre." "Adelante amigo." And greeting a recognizable young homie, like, "Was up foo? Did you hear about the car crash last night by the liquor store? A young mother was pushing her stroller?" Our language transcends and evolves and ruptures time periods and histories. When we speak, we do it in our twisted tongue, tangled trabalenguas.

Our stories are told in the bold and brazen graffiti-scrawled letters of who was here and who has passed away. Too many young Chicanos with RIP slogans. "Pinche desmadre that he died too soon." "Y su abuela couldn't believe that his ñieto died before her." Her strength is wrapped around her like a warm rebozo on a cold morning. But now she wears her black veil of sadness. This mujer india has birthmarks and scars on her back that tell stories of how she crossed the desierto wearing solamente sus huaraches. She survived rape from the coyote, abuse from her husband, and multiple miscarriages. And now she has to pay respect to her nineteen-year-old ñieto. This grandmother of indigenous features and a wrinkled face of knowledge. Her hands like fragile dry leaves, but today they still smell of this morning's masa as she fingers her rosary while praying to the Virgen. Never learned to read but can tell you about the movement of the stars and of remedies and about the beautiful hummingbirds that would visit her in the spring. She can tell you about survival. And resiliency. And sadness. And love.

The graphic and raw stories are immortalized in the vibrant colors of the murals by young men and women self-taught, porque para que voy al museo cuando tengo el arte en mi corazon. Pa que chingados voy to the galleries when my inspirations are in the middle of the street. I can hear the sounds of paleteros and car horns. The sound of music blasts from all directions. I can smell the street tacos and lonchera trucks. Y chales con la pinche jura. Trucha homie. Watch my back while I finish the outline of this mural. Chiflame cuando veas la pinche chota.

Cus all I want to do tonight is drink a 40 and pour some for the dead homies. I want to smack the shit out of the Donald Trump pinche piñata. And splatter its insides all over the place because I do not recognize your wall. Cus no border can stop the flow of water or blood or humanity. You build it. We will come. Because there is no border. Mi gente vive en los files y en los campos and the ghettos and the mobile home parks and the slums and apartment complexes and the barrios. We live in downtown projects under city lights. This is Occupied America. I don't have to leave or go anywhere cus this is home. This is Aztlan.

We are the victims of a violent history. Of bloodshed and barbed wire gouging the skin
ripping flesh while chasing the American dream.

But our stories are also of future dreams. Of seeing our loved ones once again with a warm long overdue embrace of love. Cus no words need to be spoken in this act.

Because our stories are of survival. And resiliency. And sadness. And love.

Sounds Ringing in My Head

It is the annoying muffled, static during your favorite
      television show.
It is the sound of hushed prayers in a church pew, almost
      losing faith.
It is the sound of a hungry young child wanting more,
the sound of an empty, growling stomach.

It is the sound of the long unemployment line
      and mumbled angers, "cus this shit better get better"
the sound of an eviction notice on my apartment door
the sound of gurgling warm water cracking on old pipes
      before showering
the sound of an empty cereal box being shaken
the sound of nasty leftover food being microwaved
the sound of envelopes with final notice in the mailbox and
      not a check in sight.

It is the sound of cracked whip of the belt on young flesh
the sound of the slap on the young mother's face from her
      man who loves her and she believes it
the sound of dogs barking in the streets—all night and all day
the sound of sirens and nearby screams—all night and all day.

It is the sound of "Fuck" from your lips when police is
      tracking you.
It is the sound of a young brother's face slammed on a police
      cruiser
the sound of a knee cracking his ribs while holding him down
      on the asphalt street.

It is the sound of the baton on his lower back after he squirms
and gasps for air.

We hold our breaths. It is that sound.

It is the suspenseful sound of a phone call piercing the middle
of the night no one wants to answer.

We inhale.

We exhale.

The anticipation is agonizing.

It is that sound.

The House on the Other Side

On the other side
you can see plenty of Lexuses and Rolexes
and have as much sex as you can handle.

You can take a dip in a large Los Angeles pool
in your mansion that sits atop a hill
surrounded by jungle like trees and manicured shrubs.
You might even spot a colorful toucan perched on a large
        branch
or an iguana bathing in the sun.

You can slip and slide on the marble floors
and lie around in your expensive robe.
You can take long naps in sheets of thousand count that smell
        like fresh flowers.
You can take puffs from your Cuban cigar
and sip on fine whisky while lounging by your outdoor
        fireplace.
At night you can gaze at the nearby stars through your
        skylight.

I used to be inside this mansion.
Because I cleaned the mess
made the beds
mopped the floors
I even had a key to the outside gate.

But just below, there is a house on the other side
that most ignore

where there are carpet stains
and cigarette burn holes on couch cushions
unfinished puzzle pieces and hot wheels lay scattered on the
          floor
broken cabinets are littered with mostly empty cereal boxes
          and canned food
an occasional cockroach or a small mouse roams freely inside
          the house.
there is an old console television with a signal that comes in
          and out
the fridge is mostly empty with a bucket of leftover chicken
and an old pizza box
half open gallon of milk
and four bottles of Bud Light.

Outside this home you can still hear a mother
calling for her teenage son up the street.
Driveways are littered with junked cars
and the air is filled with smells of burnt rubber and gasoline
and spilt oil.
You can smell the chicken waste in the backyard.
Rottweiler and German Shepherds lay in their own mess.

I know this home,
          this home below the mansion, on the other side
still belongs to me
still lives in me
because I sat on the linoleum floor
as I practiced my penmanship
and drew in coloring books.
I dreamt of being an artist.

My crayon marks are still on the wall.
I still have a key to this house.

I still think of both homes. I get nostalgic and sad.
While I was in the mansion, I dreamt of many beautiful things
        and thought of my escape
and while I lived on the house below, I dreamt about the
        mansion on top of the hill.

From Fathers to Sons… and to Their Sons

Part 1: My Father

My father has never said I love you.
And I have been his son for a long time.
As a child he never kissed me goodbye
or attended a parent conference
or even read a report card.
He never learned to hug his children.
Even today his hugs are awkward and clumsy.
And are more like a sideways lean and pat on the shoulder.

Did he teach me how to tie my shoelaces?
Ride a bike?
Throw a ball?
Did he talk to me about sex?
Or teach me how to talk to girls?

What do you think?

My father showed different emotions—
anger
frustration
disappointment
bitterness.
And he was filled with this rage on most days.
His machismo was directed at my mother on most occasions
as he dragged her across the kitchen floor
and hurled obscenities at her
while we screamed and cried.

He stole our innocence
with vulgar and hateful words that pierced our eardrums.
The belt whippings left welts on our skin that burned like salt
          on fresh wounds.
They became etched like tattoos for weeks.

He screamed,
 "You need to stop crying cabron. I didn't hit you that hard."
"Get up. Stop being a pussy."
"If you don't stop crying, I'm going to give you something to
          really cry about."
"Vales una chingada."
This is how I became a man.

Part 2: My Son

My firstborn was a son. He was a surprise.
I have learned to love him on my own
without books
or advice from the older men in my family
who drank Bud with buds
whose best friends were Jose Cuervo and Don Julio
who drank their asses off on weekends
screamed and beat their own wives and children
went to church on Sundays to feel better,
and repeated the cycle the following weekend.

I miss my son at a young age.
I want my son to be little again
to narrate about his day in the elementary school playground
to tell me about the story he read in class
and the schoolboy crush he has on a girl with long curls.

I wish he could run into my arms again
or sit on my lap.
I wish I can kiss his chubby cheeks
or throw a baseball with him
or read him a book at bedtime.

My son has become a young man.
He has made countless mistakes
and I worry about him.
But I know he cannot be a man without these lessons.
He has flaws and imperfections.
I am not ashamed of him.
So, I tell him that things will be okay
and this too shall pass.

Part 3: My Reconciliation

I cannot be a hypocrite.
I have been prey to my own weaknesses.
I will never confess these
not in a poem
or a song
or a canvas.
I have secrets that will die with me.

There is no practice or rehearsal
in being a father.
I have only one chance to do it right.

I am challenged every day.
My son is vulnerable… as I am.
I am traumatized by my father's words and actions

as they pulsate in my head every time my son makes a
      mistake.

I was a pendejo more than once.
I felt the kick from his boot on my ass more than once.
I cried after the slap to back of my head more than once.

A worn-out leather belt raised me.
Curse words raised me.
Disappointment raised me.
Anger raised me.

Tough love raised me.

But in raising my son
      I would rather love
than be tough.

Drunk Tios

Hardened men pour out when the sun sets.
Battle-bruised, hunched over, and coughing up residue
after inhaling dangerous chemicals
from working in unsafe conditions and poor ventilation.

These men—our fathers
                              our tios
                                        compadres
factory workers
mechanics
ditch diggers
gardeners
piscadores
cement sewer pipe builders
roofers.

Dust on their backs.
Sweat on their foreheads.
Permanent oil smudges between nails and skin
and muscles and veins bulge from their arms.

Their cracked
          calloused
                    cut
                              bruised
                                        pinched
                                                  battered hands
have rarely held a pencil
but now the grasp a 40-ounce in a brown paper sack.

The first bitter taste of alcohol
burns their throat
but slides like honey.
They listen to some old Spanish songs that crack from muffled
        speakers
                of their old, beat-up Silverado in their driveway.
This quiet moment of peace
before walking into the chaos of the house.
Because children need new school clothes and backpacks
and their mujeres need new shoes.

Other tios stumble into old cantinas
dance with ficheras
smoke half a pack of cigarettes
and slump over the bar.

And past the lingering, burning clouds of smoke
among chatter, laughter, and loud norteño music
his sobrino musters all the courage of a scrawny freckled-faced
        mocosillo,

"Vamos tio. My tia is waiting for you in the car. Esta enojada"

Tio is finally laying across the ripped back seat
of the passed down Toyota Tercel.
The stench of alcohol and cigarettes permeates the car.
Between sniffles and deep breaths
and whimpering like a scolded child, he says,
        "I love you mujer. Perdoname."
        "I know. I won't go again."
        "No. I don't have a girlfriend."

His words etching promises . . . again.
Tears are streaming down his face.
     And for once
       he is shredding his masculinity like peeling layers of old
          skin from his working hands.

Makes Me Wanna Holler

"Make me wanna holler / The way they do my life."
—Marvin Gaye

There is no reason for it—
and sometimes there are too many reasons.

I got this burning 'n yearning desire inside of me
ready to explode
      burst out melodies of screams.
A deep hummin' holler for the garbage can winos
street scene peddlers
corner store philosophers
for the old-reformed disco pimp daddy hustler
      still got the slow-mo dip in his cool stride
spilling nonchalant wisdom in loose lyrical words from paper
      sacks
weaving stories into perfect braids.

No Motown grooves or singing the blues
this is a straight-out holler
and I'm gonna go tell it to every mountain.

To reach back into the depths of my anguish
and belch out a thunderous holler
a roaring roller-coaster of a roar
that echoes through valleys and caves
and shudders volcanoes
for the past hurt

the future rejections
      absent apologies
           broken promises.

For my father's belt slashes and whips and screams
with a, "No llores. Los hombres no lloran."
Yet, I was still a child.

On most nights, I walked on a tightrope, on tiptoes
avoiding his gaze and machismo cold stares.

I need to holler, just to holler
for his penetrating etched words in the cellblocks of my mind.
 "Because men don't hug. Men aren't supposed to be that
      close."
He was too clumsy to hug,
let alone whisper words of love
or nalgadas disguised as cariños.

I couldn't cry when the baseball hit me across my cheekbone
when I fell off the bike and scraped a gash,
     clean took off my skin off of my knee.
I couldn't cry when my mother screamed for help while he
     dragged her across the floor.
I couldn't cry when one of my best friends overdosed in the
     back alley.
I couldn't cry when my tia died of cancer.

So, I need to holler
for every single religious guilt.
A holler for the dark secrets
and cobwebbed-infested skeletons

and repressed confessions.

I need to holler for the bomb squad intellectuals of the streets
the poets and the rappers and the rhymers.
They be stringin' and strummin' rhymes in cohesion
feastin' and freestylin' it in their own free speech lingo-logues
pleading for our sanity.

I'm trying to escape   to escape
to feel safe
secure in this world
because I need that unconditional mother love.
Her love is a sacrifice.

Just one final punctuating holler with an exclamation point!
To remove my clothes
get naked
self-disclose
to relieve me of my pain
                    guilt
                              and repressed male pride
                                        bullshit.

Cus I have carried the trauma of toxic masculinity.
Cus I can't be a pussy. Cus I need to be a man.
Cus I cannot show my weakness
        or someone is liable to put a knife in my throat.

I need a straight out, one time, one shot, no chaser kinda
        holler
for being born
and one for living

yet, not feeling alive.

A long echoing holler that never stops
a humongous shoutout
a big holler
a hundred hollers all at once
to echo and make continuous beats of hollers
a loud wailing rhythm of vodoo hodoo
and Hip-Hop hollers.

Hollering at the top of my lungs
cus it feels so good to holler.
Holler so damn loud make' me go deaf
holler and keep on hollering
holler till I can't no more.

     Then take a pause. . . Take a deep breath
and holler some more.

And I am not talking about a whimper
     or a sob
          or a pre-mature pout
               or a trickled tear
          a scream   a painful wail
but a motherfuckin' real holler.

Holler for no reason at all.
Holler for every reason.
Holler just to holler.
Any kind of holler.
So many hollers all at once.

Just one final erupting
      orgasmic
          climatic
              volcanic
                  powerful
                      earthshaking
                          trembling
holler that makes everyone quiver and squeal
and run for cover.

Just hear me holler,

AAAAAAAAAAAAAHHHHHHHHHHHHHHHHHHHH
HHHHHHHHHHHHHHH!!!!!!!!!

Writing for Freedom

*"They ask me what I'm writing for? /
I'm writing to show you what we fighting for"*
                                        —Talib Kweli

Got myself tongue-tied
cus I got a lot to say
but I'm a wicked son of Satan
hot air is blazing fire out of my lungs
my words are oozing lava out of my mouth
my spit is stinging with grandfather pass-me-down wisdom.

It's difficult to catch up to my thoughts
better catch them before they evaporate into yesterday's
        memories or afterthoughts.
Lyrics be sampled on old tunes.
I got a freaky thing on my mind
and it ain't no woman this time.
Something more like freedom
scribbled, tagged, and re-tagged on concrete graffiti walls.
Gotta let it shine
con safos style
cus I need to feel what is real.

Been losing touch for days.
Been closing-off tight too many years.
Swallowing and repressing my shit.
So, I usually lie twice a day.
But not today,

too many are watching my back.
And oh, how it bleeds.
The wound ruptures and screams.
Puss circles and oozes out of gangrene pores.
Didn't know the truth would hurt so bad.
And oh, how it hurts.
But it's pumping the funk.
Blasting the blood out of yo speakers.

Yo, it's like I'm writing for freedom.
Didn't know I had to protest
and chant slogans in large lines
with screams of anger to protect the faith.
It cost a heavy price today.
I'm lucky I have nine lives.
I'm trying to survive.
Can't let my children see me cry.

Pac wonders if heaven is a ghetto.
I'm wondering if hell is on earth.

I'm supposed to be celebrating my firstborn's birth
but telephone lines, TV newsman, and radio reporters are
        screaming of a holocaust.
A terrorist genocide.
Explosions shook me frantic like seizures and convulsions.
Black smoky clouds
are raining blazing fires and concrete, rubble and asphalt
        storms.
Screams are silenced by echoes of other screams
and the sirens scream.

Hip-Hop, you are my love.
My escape from this chaos.
And I put my secret words to it.
If I can't embrace you when I'm hating
then this shit ain't real.

I just never knew I had to fight to keep you.
But now I know I can't take this for granted.
Like freedom should be contagious,
but too many use it and abuse it.
How can we reflect and recognize
that a blank notebook is not your slavery?
Scribble like there is no tomorrow.
Till your hand aches, throbs, and pains
till you're writing mental block is cast away
keeping ya head up, keeping you sane.

Terrorists can't spill yo family tree-blood
keep you alive
even after the lynch mobs
public hanging
border crossing rapes
internment and reservation camps.
Survival is your revival.
A song of redemption.
I'm singing the blues.
I'm still singing the blues.
Never will I get over this rage.
History is pain.
I can't forget about it.

It's why I'm writing for freedom.

Black and Brown

Brothas and carnales ARE Hip-Hop!
But too many think Mexican MCs ain't real.
But raza been in since the creation.
The genesis has even grown
       in the marrow of my bones.
This is my inception.
My conception.
And it's more than a dream.

I sucker punch punks.
I ain't even drunk.
Bad taste in my mouth
like stanky funk.
Like love and sex in momma's garage.

Stories of ghetto dreams.

Gunshots pierce the sky.
Grandmothers' rosaries keeping vatos alive.
Father working overtime.
Momma riding the bus past Midnight.
We smoke peace pipes.
We up all night.
Wish I was a cat and lived nine lives.

Gunshots and sirens unrest.
Yellow tape surrounds a bloody mess.
White sheets cover blood and flesh.

But out of the muck and mess
walks in a beauty with a fine dress.
Hearts are caressed.
Crumbled papers become fresh.
On walls of graffiti love is professed.
Songs and poems lullaby babies to rest.

Fake rappers need to digress.
Flows are a mess.
Haters need to rest.

Reveal and express
what has been repressed.

Americans are jealous of our music
piñatas
lowriders
chilaquiles
tequila
and street tacos.
We put that shit on the map.
All over USA.

We didn't even
cross borders.
We brought order to this chaos and disorder.
So, I cross my t's and dot my I's
cus this is my new world order.

Brothers and carnales—Why the hell are we fightin'?
We both hustlin'.
        We both grindin'.

We both survivin'.

We rummagin' through trashcans
collectin' aluminum cans in black Glad bags.
Trying to taste a piece of the pie.
If I pursue this happiness, is it worth it to die?

We held hands together.
We protested together.
We boycotted together.
We danced together.
We made art together.

But now we slap our women.
Leave our children.
Sip on 40's
and scope out the shorties.
Fill prisons together.
Lose brothers to violence together.
We used to pray together.

Real ghetto shit.
This is our story
of survival and pain.
Erasing the doubt
and the drought
cus I am praying for rain.
Ain't never even touch or slang rock
but I dance on the concrete block.

Music is my heel.
Rhyming is for real.

Words are fuckin' real.

I write to feel
and to erase the pain   confess   and to heal.

A Long Line of Pachucos

—dedicated to Jose Montoya, poet, artist, activist

Creo en un solo vato,
son of a pachuco zoot-suiter,
who threw down with the servicemen.
So, hey noble Nobel Prize Paz,
give us peace.
Por favor, please.

I do not want to enter your labyrinth,
I hate solitude.
You see,
I know who I am.

El vato de Fourth Street—
Chavo—
a smooth vato
with a voice like a whisper
gets down with some firme murals.
Has a tecato for a carnal,
who drank his sorrows away
in a dark cell in San Quentin
after Penal Code 187.

Dreams of the return of Quetzalcoatl,
un solo dios,
creador de cielo y tierra, uvas y naranjas,
picked by Chicano farmworkers,
en los files de Califas.

His parents both worked the fields
skin becoming like roasted cacahuates,
hands dry like leather,
children of the Fifth Sun,
faces, deep brown
like the earth they toil.

That's him,
with a clean white, wifebeater
tucked into pleated khakis
and a paño around his forehead.
Hijo de un campesino,
who lost his primavera
in the Spring of '91
and became a man
with the pretty daughter of the vieja,
ciega from one eye.

He kicks it down on Lemon and Eighth,
with Spooky and Flaco.
Known as Homeboy Street
or Pachuco Row.
Homies for life.
The juras nightmare
and nobody fucks with that barrio.

Barrio is named Dolores.
History runs deep.
Long before grandfathers came home on horseback,
celebrating the cosecha,
and savoring frijoles,

tortillas de maiz,
chile rojo,
from the palate of their mouths.
And shouts
with shots of Tequila
for the defeat of the pinche Gachupíns.

Long before big cities,
streetlights,
corner malls
with a hair salon,
a dry cleaner,
and Chinese Fast Food.
Gentrification has tried to bury the barrio.

Homies are just kicking it tonight at the park
and the jainas cruise by,
"Wanna party with the vatos?"
"Pos les go."
Porque chingados why not?
Ultimadamente we ain't got shit to do,
on a Friday night.

Ñietos de abuelitas,
wrapped up in rebozos of a thousand years,
passed down like a generational quilt
first offered by Tonantzin to an indigenous mother.
Who makes the best flour tortillas,
children taking them off the comal,
spreading butter and sprinkles of salt.

And the vatos and the jainas

cruise down the dark Boulevard on the '69 Impala.
Smoke-filled car,
hiding the beers underneath the seat,
windows rolled down
and Brenton Wood is jamming through the speakers.

Spooky in the back seat,
throwing a placaso
on La Gina's thin neck.
and Flaco, eyes squinting,
head slowly grooving,
blowing marihuana smoke
out the window,
spreading noticias of their existencia.

And tonight, Chavo remembers his carnal
who taught him about art and graffiti
and spilled wisdom about Aztec gods and goddesses
and pride in the barrio.
"And don't let the pinche gabachos take your shit."

Cruise till the end of night.
Stopping at no borders,
coyotes are bringing brown brothers and sisters
across to join them.
No Mexican INS agents around. Fuck ICE.
Any wall can be scaled.
No fence can hold the sea back.
And everything is firme,
cus this is their turf,
and they are the O.G. Pachucos.

FOR BROKEN-HEARTED FOOS

I Felt the Lowest

I have spent whole entire days alone.
And I thought that was normal.
Something inside me gnawed at me, inch by inch.

On many days I was haunted by muffled sounds
or a monotone droning in my head.
Other times I was punished by a migraine ringing in my ear.

On many nights, I felt the lowest.
I have cried quietly like an infant
and curled up into a ball into myself.

Until I felt the touch of your hands.
Your fingertips lifted me up like a feather into the sky.
Your lips graced my eyes lightly.

And your silent sweet voice
forgave me
and whispered in my ears.

You taught me to find pieces of myself.
Slowly, I am gluing my broken, scattered self . . .
        And making me whole again.

One day at a time.
One piece at a time.
I am learning to love myself again.

And . . . now I feel the magic of music singing in my bones.

The sound is brilliant and joyful.

And … I see new colors that I hadn't seen before.
I see lights that others don't.
Not sure where they come from or what they mean.
But they are beautiful.

And I no longer feel lonely.

Take My Hand

Take my hand.
You lead
and I will follow you, never letting go.

One day I will learn to be alone.
Walk the empty sidewalk
to find you.

I will take comfort as I imagine you next to me.
I will watch my breath evaporate into the cold chilly night
and stare at the stars at night.

I will learn to love
and to take risks
and to overcome
        the pains and remains of my broken heart.

Take my hand.
And I will follow.
Squeeze my hand tightly.
So, the warmth of your hand gives me comfort.

Lay down with me.
I want to watch you sleep
        and imagine your fleeting thoughts.
I want to see the beauty of your dreams.
I want to touch what you see.
And travel back to your innocent times.
But never leave my side.

Take my hand.
Lead me to strange places.
Walk with me in the rain.
Take slow steps.
Tread lightly.

Take my hand,
and I will follow.

But never let me go
and be gentle with my timid heart.

If I Had You Next to Me

If I had you next to me
I would not follow form and function
nor principle or protocol.
I would follow my desire
and impulse and instinct and urges.

I would claw my way to you.
My hunger would swell
and I would rip and tear my pleasures.

I would not shyly touch your hand.
But I would grab it and lead it.

C'mon don't be so sweet. Don't be so shy.
Do you envy my untethered desires?
I am not sorry for my sloppy and messy kisses.

I would not whisper sweet things in your ear.
I would smother your innocent face.
My screams of your name would burn your tender skin.

I would not kiss your neck softly
but l would bite it and mark it.
Red welts,
purple, bloody, and bruised teeth marks
would be on your slender neck for days.

I will not take my pleasurable time
but I will fiercely take advantage of your weakness and

vulnerability.

Sometimes I just want to be guttural.
Sometimes I want to be careless. Reckless.
I want to lose consciousness with you.

I want to ravage you.
I want to devour you
teeth sharpening, biting through soft tissue
famished
ravenous.

Like a feral and untamed animal
in the wild of the night.

If I Could Tell You How Much I Love You

If I could tell you how much I love you—
>   I would say that I want to accidentally see you walk
>   across my path.
>   Interrupt my train of thought.
>   Come into focus of my blurred vision
>   and see you smile as you recognize me.

I would take my insides
>   and present them on your lap
so you can see my feelings float around like happy butterflies
then drizzle and sprinkle your naked skin
like scattered confetti.

I wish you knew that while I sleep I train my subconscious to
create dreams about you. In my dream you are sleeping
peacefully and I am watching you. I am following your silent
breathing. Your sighs. Your reliefs. Inhales and exhales. It is
the most pleasant image.

If I could tell you how much I love you—
I would say that your eyes remind me of something magical. I
wish I could drink the sweet and intoxicating liquid inside your
mysterious eyes.
Just the mere touch of your hands on my skin sends me into a
possessed spirit and I am all yours.

I would tell you that I see my hand and stare at it. I trace the
marks and spots and tiny scars on it from childhood years.

But I wish I was staring at your hand. Holding the gentleness of it and tracing each of your fingers.

If I could tell you how much I love you—
I would tell you that I wish you lived across the street. From my window, I would watch you comb your hair.
At night, I would throw pebbles at your window and whisper your name. We would then sneak outside and lay blankets under a large tree. We would watch the leaves sway back and forth and dance gently. We would trace the path of all the stars in the night sky. It would be such a lovely night.

And you and I would be kids again. And we would be innocent again.

And when I tell you that I love you, I would also tell you how good it feels when you look at me that way.

Some Sad News

I told her some sad news
that I had met a woman
     met her eyes
     met her lips.

That she smelled fresh
     and tasted sweet
     and her hands felt different than hers.

I told her that this woman made me cry.
     She hurt me and caused me pain.
     And made me feel anguish more than anyone.

But she also helped me rest
     and dream and imagine and feel
     and the angels were floating in my head.

She listened to my screams.
And the cracking in my voice.
And she put her ears against my chest
to hear the sound of my breathing
and the quiet murmurs of my beating heart.

With her fingers she traced the scars on my back
the wrinkles on the corners of my eyes
the blemishes of my skin
and she touched my mouth with her fingertips.

There was a fire in my eyes

a longing in my chest
and a desire in the marrow of my bones.

Nothing hateful seethed from her eyes.
No vile words exited from her lips.
Her mouth was perfect.
And she had a secret mystery.

But she went home to him.
And I went home to her.
        To tell her some sad news about this woman I met.

Our Love Was Secret

"Moving on seems harder to do/When the one that you love/Moves faster than you"

—*Khalid*

Our love is secret.
Like hushed prayers.
Like a whisper, soft as a feather.

It is volatile, mostly.
Like open wounds and battle scars.
Like restless oceans.
Like fault lines bulging
        and erupting into dangerous earthquakes.

In your absence I reminisce on what I miss.

I miss the scar on your cheek.
I miss how the wind carried your voice to reach me.
I miss the sound of your laughter.
And the warmth of your breathing.
I miss the place where your neck meets your shoulder.
I even loved seeing you cry
        and collecting your tears
because you looked so beautiful when you were sad.

I wait for you to return to me
to feel you one last time
to say one more thing to you.

But you are now in the embrace of another.
My whispers no longer reach your ears
and the pleasant scent of your aroma has disappeared.
Even the tender feeling of your touches
        escapes my memory.

I wish you could have left me more than wounds.
I wish I could have given you more than words.
My love was never enough to keep you.
And there is a sad heart inside my rib cage.

Our love was fleeting.
Our love was a tiny moment . . .

Forgetting you will be long and agonizing.

Just Because

"You can't break my heart 'cause I/ Was never in love"
—Odesza

Just because I am alone, doesn't mean that I feel lonely
just because I feel hopeless, doesn't mean that I've lost hope.

Just because I'm lost, doesn't mean I'm losing
just because I have no home, doesn't mean I have nowhere to
     go.

Just because I'm shattered, doesn't mean I can't be whole
     again
just because it's dark, doesn't mean I can't see the light.

Just because I'm drinking, doesn't mean I'm numb
just because there are gray, overcast clouds above my head,
     doesn't mean I'm depressed.

Just because it hurts, doesn't mean I can't get over the pain
just because you wounded me, doesn't mean I can't heal.

Just because your name echoes inside me, doesn't mean I can't
     forget you
just because I'm crying, doesn't mean it's for you.

And because the night is clear, I can finally be a star.

I Am Sorry

"Curse of us sinning and healing/
I do all of this hoping she'll see me"
     —Dermot Kennedy

I am sorry.
I don't want this to be another sad poem.

Sometimes I want to float among the clouds.
See you from afar.
Spot you as a speckle.
Then bring you into focus
as a tiny and precious little treasure.

I have heard of love and the stars.
And of the ocean and waves.
And of birds and flowers.
And of rainbows and sunshine.

But nothing prepared me for the lingering pain.
Because when you are gone
I only smell burnt trees
and see dry grass.
I taste spoiled fruit
and only hear broken glass on sidewalks.

I feel the heat and the cold.
The burns of fresh cuts and bruises.
And I wish I could photoshop my heart

to cover up these scars that you left me with.

I am sorry that I am vulnerable and weak.
I never meant to be this way.
I am sorry that I am selfish
to want you … now at this moment.

But this empty hole makes me suffer.
And I want to utter words I am afraid to say.
So, I try to remember the sound of your voice
        sweet, soft, soothing delicate, like lace
pleasant like a deep inhale and a slow meditative exhale.
And I try to doodle and draw pictures of your hands
and write similes about your eyes
and metaphors of your smile
so, these memories can be engraved in me.

So, wrap your arms around me.
Feel me like I feel you.
Love me like I love you.
Because I am exhausted from the endless drives with the
        windows rolled down
                playing sad music.
I am overwhelmed from the sleepless nights in my lonely
        room
                while writing shitty poems about you.

And maybe you are not the most beautiful.
But your laughter is.
And I am the happiest person when I witness this moment.

And I wish you knew that when I hear your name at random,

I quiver like crunchy dry leaves.
Your voice is music to slow dancing.
Like gentle chimes on a breezy day.

I wish you knew that your face is a beautiful memory . . .
                                                    every day.
Your eyes ignite fireworks in me ready to explode.
And a rush of emotions
makes me nauseous like rainbows circling inside me.

And I wish you knew that thoughts about you
are always dripping at the tip of my pen.

Show Her the Stars

"But are we all lost stars/
Trying to light up the dark?"
—Gregg Alexander, New Radicals

She will be sad and the pain will linger.
And the scars will show their fleshy hurt time after time.
Her sobbing heart will leap out of her chest.
But show her your wounded heart in the palm of your hands
        because you hurt . . . when she hurts.
Show her with your actions to trust, to let go, to be vulnerable.

Hold her hand and guide her to frightening places.
Embrace her tightly when she is scared
and even at random moments.
Lick the falling tears when they trickle down her cheek.
Comfort her with patience till she sighs from relief.
Be gentle with her soul because her past was trampled
      scattered like puzzle pieces
          and crumbled like fall leaves under footsteps.

While her head rests on your chest,
gaze at the celestial night sky.
Hold her fingertips in your hands
and connect the dots between the stars.
Give them wonderful names.
Stare deeply into her eyes
so you can read what's inside her thoughts.
Take her to the places she has only dreamt of.

Touch her gently.
Send chills down her spine and goose bumps down her legs.

Travel the world together.
See untainted magical lands.
Invent a secret language.
Grace her lips gently with yours.
Run your fingers lightly on her untouched body.
Dance and invent music together.

Lift her soul to the heavens
and make her the most glorious person in the sky.
Make her feel so light that she can float among the clouds.
Make the earth shatter.
Make mountains tremble and roar.
Make oceans whip and become restless and powerful.
Make the night sky blaze and glitter with fiery falling stars.

I Used to Work at a Liquor Store

I used to work at a liquor store when I was young.
Stocking and stuffing the ice cooler with beer bottles and
          aluminum cans,
I was mesmerized by the colorful liquor bottles behind the
          counter.
Too expensive for a poor kid.
My favorite was the dark liquid in a green bottle.

. . . And tonight, I think of you.
I remember the laughter erupting from our throats.
Maybe because of the many drinks I shared with you.
Yours were fruity and colorful and sweet.
And mine were dark and sour and bitter.
Whiskey that burned my throat
but I was happy because I would see two of you when I drank.

It would be nice if you thought of me tonight on my birthday.
Called me.
Even though I hate birthdays
because they remind me of my sadness
and no one understands it.

Except the falling star in the night sky.
The solo guitar strumming in the early hours.
The heavy ripe fruit that falls from its tree
only to be forgotten or trampled.
The alcoholic street vagrants.
The woman fingering her change while waiting for a bus.

I am all the sad music
crushing in my bones.
I am the promises from your lips that never came.
I am the end of the book that never should be finished.

I wait for you
again, and again
night after night
if only to hear your voice so that it soothes my loneliness.

Tonight . . . I might forgive you for the hurt.
I might even let you hold my hand
to watch our bare feet leave imprints on the damp sand.

But you will not call.
I know this.
So tonight, I will let the alcohol burn my throat again.
One drink to remember.
And one drink to forget.

COMING UP

I'm an Emotional Mess

"All Writing is Confession"
—Cherrie Moraga

I'm an emotional mess. Every day is a fuckin' test. When I get so high, I'm so high. When I get so low, I'm so low. Today is a low-low day.

This feeling comes up from the pit of my stomach. And it climbs up my throat. But it gets stuck there. I can't release it or push it down. I can't vomit it or cough it up. It just stays there like permanent phlegm or green bile eating away at any tiny, good feelings I have left in me.

And then I begin to think about so many overwhelming things. And there is no calm left in me. Just this fuckin' sadness that weighs down on my shoulders like dark gray heavy clouds.

I still have dreams of Satan terrorizing me. You can even ask my mother. I hear her pray for me at night. In my dreams I am 12 years old running from demons and evil spirits. My brother told me to confront an evil spirit, but I am terrified, so I run away. I think I am experiencing sleep paralysis because I am totally immobile when I wake up. I am stiff and exhausted and cannot make out where I am. I am out of breath. While awake, I hear noises. It's all in my fuckin' head. I turn on the lights for an hour till I calm down and try to think of simple things like my peanut butter and jelly sandwiches and potato chips for lunch. Rides on school buses and ice cream summer afternoons.

If I show you my weaknesses or my fears or my worries, am I less of a man? Am I a pussy if I admit to you that I've cried on the long drives to work? I have had lonely fits of rage and self-doubt for no apparent reasons. I have stayed inside my car for hours in parking lots not ready to buy my weekly groceries or face other humans. I have buried myself in guilt and remorse for several years asking questions about complex things that have no answers.

No. I am not miserable. I just have random bouts of sadness. I am brokenhearted about a lot of things. I experience loneliness more often now and it really sucks to eat alone. I talk to myself regularly. My heart feels heavy like post-COVID, and my lungs are working overtime.

I stopped seeing my therapist. I think I should go back. He was friendly, but maybe I should just have some beers and shots with my friends in a dark bar because that shit costs less. My children say I should move back because we're still friends, but it's a complicated mess that I caused and it's too late to clean up. Plus, it's too difficult to unsee or unhear the things I have seen or heard in the last few years.

Sometimes I wanna curl up into a ball with my anger and
       disappointment.
Sometimes I hold a grudge for days.
Sometimes I wanna block people I know.
Sometimes I wanna choke them, but then I just ghost them.

I have ups and downs.
I am erratic like the ocean and the colorful hues turn into

shades of blues.
I wish I was more up than down. I wish I was more high than
  low.

I'm an emotional mess. I feel like I am a door coming off its
  hinges.
I should have a conversation with my habits and
temptations—cus I have weak thoughts of doing reckless
shit—like spending money I don't have, or drinking and
smoking, and getting HIIIIGGGGHHH. So, I could stay
HIIIGGHHHH. Cus I wanna feel HIIIGGGGHHH.

But I am afraid . . .
        of ruining relationships.

Tomorrow—I am hoping for a day full of highs.

I think back to my children.
My son creating stories at five years old.
My daughter swimming underwater at two years old.
Every day I witnessed brilliance.
That smile on my face, worth millions.

There is magic in their eyes
the truth and vision lie in my third eye.
It's time to shed the guilt
and live my life.

So, tomorrow—I will slay the day that preys
on me and my weakness.

I am tired of being an emotional mess—

of being put through a fuckin' test.

So tomorrow—I will be high.
And tomorrow—I will feel high.

Becoming

From pain to glory.
Sadness to joy.
From tears to a crooked smile.
From messy sketches to art.
From a fresh wound to a scar.
From broken strings and broken dreams
to compositions of beautiful symphonies.

Been consumed by the negative but feeling   positive.
I am turning nothing into something.
From a deep slumber of ignorance, I wake to sunshine and a
        dream.
From failed promises, I am ready to renew.
From wet dreams to grown children.
From turmoil to peace.
From chaos and disorder
        I am seeking wisdom and a new order.

I came from dirt but I will glow like a diamond.
I am down but I aspire to inspire.
I am becoming.

I am becoming.

From being sick to being healed
by a new remedy.
A thought, an epiphany
        from scribbles to poetry.
Like drunk last night to a sober reality.

I have been empty, but I will be full   filled.

I have been lost. I am trying to be found.
Because sunsets become moonlight becomes sunrise becomes
      illumination.

I am becoming.

I am becoming.

I am here.

Say Something

Bump that shit.
Make the windows rattle.
Make a screen door come off its hinges.
Make the 911 emergency sirens go off.
Make the neighborhood dogs bark like they see a cat.
Make these cats stop in their tracks.

Make teenage boys rise from their video games to witness the
      noise.
Make Wu-Tang ask, "Who bringing the muthafuckin' ruckus?"
Make old folks get up and dance.
Talk their muscles and bones into moving like they haven't for
      years then quiver to the ground.
Make flowers rise through the earth and break concrete above
      them.
Rip through the glory to reach the sunshine.

Make a loud scream.
A testament to your survival.
Make your next word mean something.
Imagine it's your last word.
Shout it at the top of your lungs.
Cus it feels so damn good to scream.
      About everything
           and about nothing.

Make alcoholics gain moments of clarity.
Make sinners crawl on their knees for repentance.
Make a new drug of words.

Make people feen for another hit of this language.
Like scripture.
Like speaking in tongues.

Bump that shit dawg.
Let me hear that battle cry.
The scream for help.
The wail from a mother looking for her missing son.
Or the pain from a lover who abandoned you.

Get to the depth of your pain and rage and sorrow and hurt
and reveal and confess
this new language of forgiveness and healing.
A language full of love.

Just say something—

but say it like you mean it.

ACKNOWLEDGMENTS

Thank you to the editors of the following journals and literary magazines, who published the following poems in the early stages or in finished form:

"Some Sad News" published by *City Works Literary Journal*, 2018

"We Wanted More" and "I Felt the Lowest" by *City Works Literary Journal*, 2020-2021

"Say Something" by *Santa Ana Literary Association*, March 2021

"Where I'm From," "From Fathers to Sons," "The House on the Other Side," and "Show Her the Stars" by *Eastside Rose*, 2021

"Hood Stories" and "Oranges at My Grandfather's House" by *The Acentos Review*, 2021

"A Little Story About My Mother" and "My Mother, the Sculptor" by *Ofrenda Magazine*, 2021

"Becoming" by *Sims Library*, 2022

"I Come from Dirt" by *San Diego Poetry Annual*, 2021-2022

"I Am Sorry" by *City Works*, 2022

"Mestizo Picadillo" and "It's a Funky World" by *Mixtape Journal*, 2022

"Drunk Tios" and "I Used to Work at a Liquor Store" by *Latin@ Literatures*, 2022

"Speaking in Tongues" by *La Raiz Magazine*, 2023

I would like to thank my grandparents, Papa Donato and Mama Juana, and Mama Lupe and Abuelo Isidoro. To my siblings—Gilberto, Ramon, Lupe, Consuelo, Mario, and Gerardo. There is poor. There is dirt poor. And there is fucked up poor. We have been there. It was not easy growing up all the time, but I think we made it—all college educated. And our father still says—"somos pinches, buenos pa nada." To my cousins, so many to name, but especially Yola, Memo, Rodrigo - thank you for the laughter, the adventures, and the honest conversations for so many years.

To my aunts and uncles, especially those that helped my parents with a room, a fridge, a bed, some cash, a meal during those early years when we first arrived from Mexico. There were so many mouths to feed, and we were always so hungry and so needy. My mother recalls the times we had no fridge so she kept milk as cold as she could, submerged in a tina (large, metal tub). But this was a task and oftentimes the milk became spoiled if the water was not changed often enough. In the middle of the night a child would wake up wanting milk, and after discovering the distinct sour odor, my father had to run to the local mercado, liquor store, or 7-11 to get fresh milk. We also had no furniture and for a dinner table, my father made a table out of a box he found in a dumpster. The boys slept on the cold floor atop a thin blanket. My two sisters slept in a tiny closet. They had plenty of room there since we had no additional clothes to hang. My mother has such a great memory but tells me to forget about this pobreza and to only think of good memories. I don't even think that was the worst of times. But I will save that for another story.

To my nieces and nephews—especially the ones who took interest in my stories and fantastic tales, sometimes made up. You are the future. Carry on tradition.

To the tiny pueblo that birthed me—if you drive too fast, you will miss it—Garcia de La Cadena, Zacatecas, Mexico. My humble beginning. One day after waking up from a nap, around dusk time, my two-year-old sister Lupe and I went to search for our mother. I was four years old. We were clutching each other's hands, looking for our mother near the arroyo where she washed clothes. We were lucky to have been found that night. Imagine. That is also another story for another time.

To my friends (and many of my cousins) who grew up on the streets of Home Gardens, our tiny neighborhood in Corona, California, our little barrio that will always breathe in us, will always live in us. You can take the boy out of the barrio, but you cannot take the barrio out of the boy. We too have ghetto dreams.

To my friends and faculty and staff from Fullerton College, Cal Poly Pomona, Cal State Fullerton, and Santa Ana College. Thank you for the opportunities and the support. Thank you for the wisdom you shared. To the many students that I have met—thank you for placing faith in me in the classroom. I hope you were inspired to write and to read. Remember, no one will read it, if you do not write it.

Thank you to MEChA and MASA at Cal Poly Pomona, for inspiring the early years of my student activism. We visited so many schools, we marched, we protested, we paid tributes, we traveled to conferences, we celebrated. Together, we honored our beautiful raza and our community.

To the many colleagues and friends (and especially the students) that I have met from The Puente Program. The workshops and trainings filled me with a passion and a new drive. Thank you especially to my partner and co-coordinator for 25 years—Reina Sanabria—we had so many great memories and in the process helped to graduate and transfer many students. Our friendship will last a lifetime.

Thank you to Alejandro Villalpando, Eduardo Valencia, and Guillermo Najar (RIP Yemito. Pinche Berdo. I miss you). We met, we read and critiqued each other's work. We planned, we designed, and finally self-published a tiny collection of poetry, Tacos de Lengua. It was a labor of love. You are my real ones. My carnales.

Thank you to Obed Silva, for the beautiful foreword and for always being authentic. My homie, my brother. We first met at a Puente conference and since then have shared meals, laughs, and love of our gente, culture, art, and books.

To my office partner at Santa Ana College for 25 years, Angelina Veyna. I will miss your stories and the many laughs we shared. I learned so much about teaching from you. I appreciate your sincerity.

To Dr. Jessica Ayo Alabi, I admire your work at Orange Coast College and in your community. You have always stayed connected to our raza. Your words are inspiring.

Much love and respect for the early review and heartfelt comments about this collection by Tomas Moniz, Matt Sedillo, and Luis J. Rodriguez.

Last but not least, thank you to Matt Sedillo, for the advice, encouragement, and support to finish this project. To David A. Romero for the creative work and the editing of this project. I look forward to moving forward with both of you. "Una mano no se lava sola" (Rodolfo Acuña).

ABOUT THE AUTHOR

Donato Martinez was born in in small pueblo, Garcia de la Cadena, Zacatecas, Mexico and immigrated into the USA at six years old. He teaches English Composition, Literature, and Creative Writing at Santa Ana College. He has also taught classes in Chicano Studies. He has been a co-coordinator of the Puente Program for 25 years. He hosts and curates many artistic events that feature poetry and music at his campus or in the community. He is also a poet and writes about his barrio experience, his community, his Chicano culture, bilingual identities, and other complexities of life. He is influenced by the sounds and pulse of the streets, people, music, and the magic of language. He has a self-published collection with three other Inland Empire poets, *Tacos de Lengua*. His work has been published by *City Works*, *East Side Rose*, *The Acentos Review*, *San Diego Poetry Annual*, *Ofrenda Magazine*, *The Mixtape Literary Journal*, *Latin@ Literatures*, and *La Raiz Magazine*. He loves the outdoors and is inspired by books, music, and his children, Gabriel and Abigail.

EL MARTILLO
PRESS

El Martillo Press publishes writers whose pens strike the page with clear intent; words with purpose to pry apart assumed norms and to hammer away at injustice. El Martillo Press proactively publishes writers looking to pound the pavement to promote their work and the work of their fellow pressmates. There is strength in El Martillo.

El Martillo Press launch 2023:

- *Touch the Sky* by Donato Martinez
- *WE STILL BE: Poems and Performances* by Paul S. Flores
- *God of the Air Hose and Other Blue-Collar Poems*
        by Ceasar K. Avelar
- *the daughterland* by Margaret Elysia Garcia
- *A Crown of Flames: Selected Poems & Aphorisms*
        by Flaminia Cruciani

To purchase these books and to keep up with new titles, visit elmartillopress.com.

CPSIA information can be obtained
at www.ICGtesting.com
Printed in the USA
BVHW050742170523
664185BV00005B/13